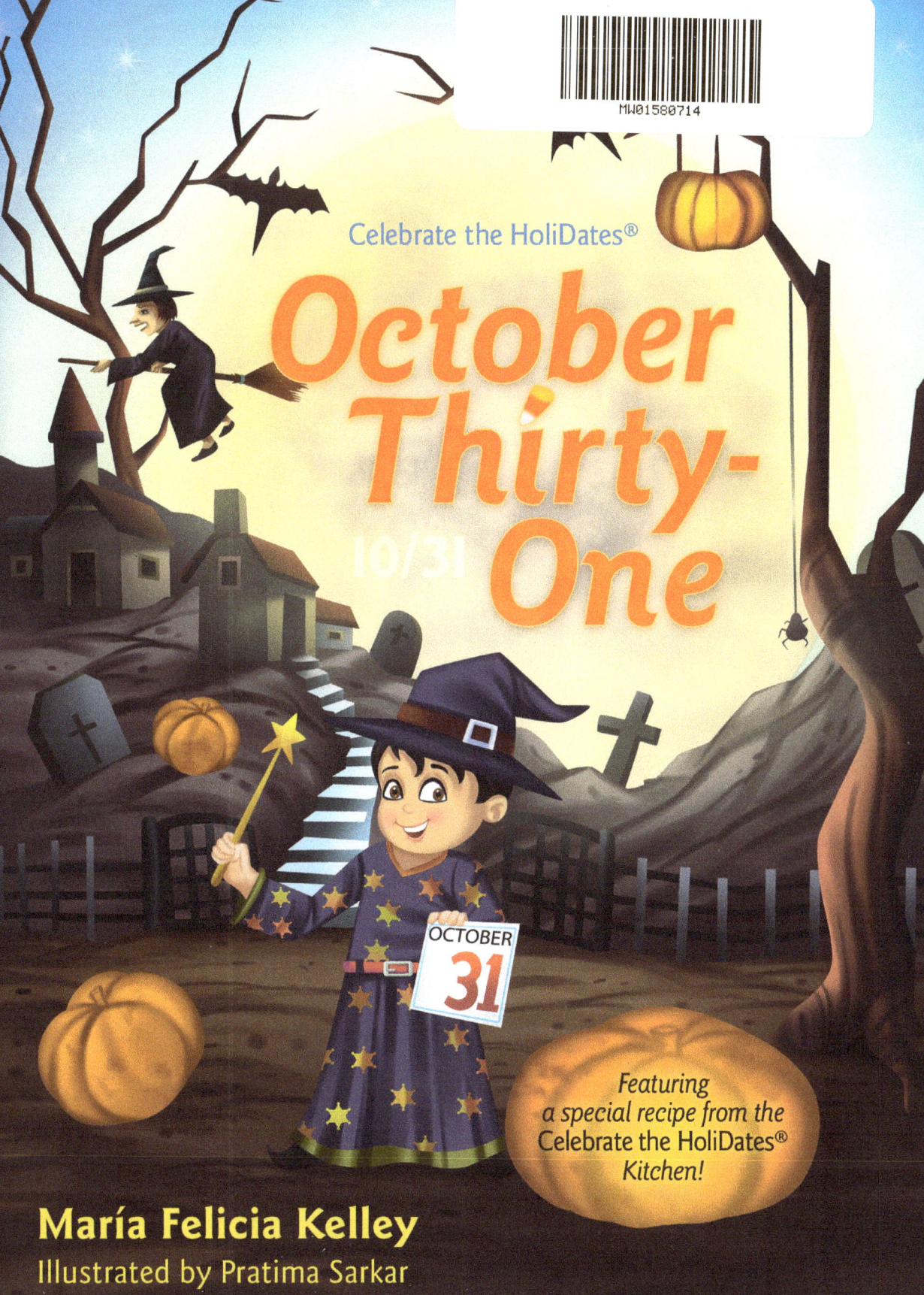

Copyrighted Material

October Thirty-One—10/31
A *Celebrate the HoliDates*® book series title

Copyright © 2021 by María Felicia Kelley. All Rights Reserved.

No part of this publication may be reproduced, stored in a retrieval system or transmitted, in any form or by any means—electronic, mechanical, photocopying, recording or otherwise—without prior written permission from the publisher, except for the inclusion of brief quotations in a review.

For information about this title or to order other books and/or electronic media, contact the publisher:

Circle7531, LLC
circle7531.com
radius@circle7531.com

ISBNs:
978-1-7355504-0-4 (hardcover)
978-1-7355504-1-1 (softcover)
978-1-7355504-2-8 (eBook)

Printed in the United States of America

Photography by Cynthia Shaffer (María Felicia's headshot, only)

Illustrations by Pratima Sarkar

Page-number (pumpkin) art created by author's youngest son, Constantine

Book design & cover finalized by 1106 Design

A Dedication to Constantine

My son, Constantine, loves holidays. He enjoys them so much he inspired my Celebrate the HoliDates® book series. The series began because Constantine is a Halloween fanatic! I wrote this book to celebrate all that the holiday means to him. He loves everything about the day and regularly tries to scare me with Halloween stories of his own. I wanted this book to be less scary and more celebratory. The goal was to bring awareness of the month of October and the date of Halloween. I wanted Constantine to become a "calendar-pro," able to pinpoint the date, no longer assuming the beginning of every month signals his favorite day is approaching ... unless, it's September rolling into October, of course.

So, this one's for you, Constantine ... Happy Halloween, with all sorts of spookiness, creepiness, and love!

—Hugs, kisses, and Halloween wishes—
from Mom

"Constantine, here.

Tiptoe with me

through each page.

I promise—it won't be too creepy."

It's a month I wait for
all year long.

It's a day that is unique.

It's a choice to be almost anything.

Four things make my day complete.

Can you guess what
those four things are?

Keep reading to find out!

October, the tenth month, arrives in autumn.

It's four weeks of fun in the fall.

Leaves change color—
from green, to red, to gold.

Its harvest moon shines
on us all.

The double-digit date
is the last day of the month...

The thirty-first is everyone's favorite.

Parades and parties happening everywhere,

Excitement overflows—
You can't contain it!

All year long I think—
What will I be?

A superhero, an animal . . .
maybe a car?

When the day gets closer,
it's still hard to pick . . .

So many costume options
there are!

With sunrise, the wait is over:

"Begin, October Thirty-One!"

Chocolates, caramels, and gummies tempt me.

I want to try each one!

As soon as night falls
it gets a little spooky.

There are skeletons, witches,
and bats;

Pumpkins carved with candlelit faces; and

Hissing scary black cats.

October Thirty-One
is trick or treat day—

An All Hallows' Eve*
called Hallowe'en!

Scares, Soul Cakes†, and candy
make my day complete—

And best of all . . . there's
the shocking, creepy cuisine!

What four things make my day complete?

HAPPY

Hallowe'en—An Eve of Allhallowtide

Allhallowtide is a Christian season—
Three prayerful days for the dead.
Beginning as a Catholic ritual,
Its influence is now widespread.

Halloween is the day before
All Saints' Day—Hallowmas—
The first day of the month of November.
All Saints' Day precedes
All Souls' Day—November 2nd—
when spirits and souls are remembered.

The 9th century Pope of Rome, Italy
Created the first All Hallows' Evening*.
"Hallowe'en" is a blend of those
three words.
'Twas an eve of saints and merrymaking.

Hallowe'en happened as
harvest-time ended—
A feast for the rich,
Soul Cakes for the poor.
Needy children without much to eat—
Begged from door-to-door.

Soul Cakes—Celtic breads decorated
with crosses made of currants—
Have roots stemming from
pre-United Kingdom.
A Spirit-moving food of the Middle Ages—
Exchanging cakes for prayers let souls
into Heaven ... and ultimate freedom.

"Knock, knock," sounded the door,
Beggar's knuckles bruised and burning.
"Master, may I have some food?
Please, sir? I am starving."

"A Soul Cake for a prayer!"
Said the wealthy man inside.
"Indeed, sir, for your loved ones' souls,
I shall pray for them with pride."

"Souling" was a house-to-house ritual—
Inspiring the modern trick or treater.
A Halloween custom that sparked
Today's neighborhood, costumed,
candy-corn eater.

Welcome to the Celebrate the HoliDates® Kitchen!

Soul Cakes[†]

Sharing Soul Cakes on "All Hallows' Eve" adds a little history to any Halloween celebration. Sing the song Soul Cakes inspired centuries ago:

> A soul, a soul, a Soul cake
> Please, good missus, a Soul cake
> An apple, a pear, a plum or a cherry
> Any good thing to make us all merry...
> —Song writer unknown

These spiced cakes are like scones with raisins. Shape them as a rounded loaf, or a small cake-like cookie.

Turn the page to check out Constantine's special Soul Cakes recipe!

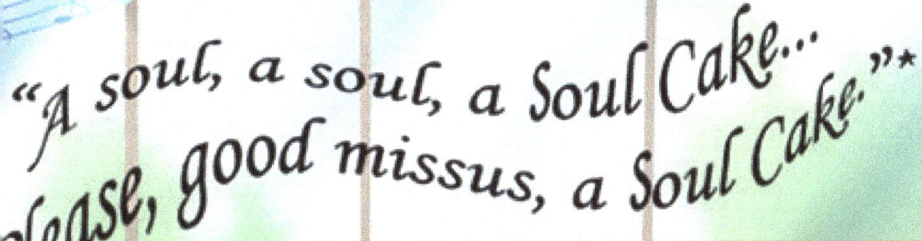

"A soul, a soul, a Soul Cake...
please, good missus, a Soul Cake."*

DIRECTIONS

1. Pre-heat oven to 350 degrees F.
2. Grease cookie sheet(s).
3. Cream butter and sugar.
4. Mix in eggs and apple cider vinegar.
5. Mix flour, salt, and ground spices in a separate bowl. Set aside.
6. Optional: Pour warm milk over saffron in small cup/bowl. Let stand five minutes.
7. Mix flour combo and butter/sugar mixture. Add milk.
8. Stir in raisins. Knead with hands.
9. Roll dough on wax paper (or pastry mat) to ½ inch thickness.
10. Cut out dough shapes using round cookie cutter or rim of glass.
11. Place dough shapes on baking sheet; mark each with an X, using tip of a butter knife.
12. Optional: Decorate X with raisins.
13. Bake for 20 minutes. Remove; cool 5 minutes; then place on cooling rack.
14. Optional: On warm cakes, sprinkle powdered sugar.

Enjoy!

Citations

Aubrey, John. *Remaines of Gentilisme and Judaisme*. 1686–87. Ed. James Britten. London: The Folklore Society, 1880. 23.

Britannica, The Editors of Encyclopaedia. "Halloween." Encyclopedia Britannica, 19 Oct. 2020, https://www.britannica.com/topic/Halloween. Accessed 29 March 2021.

Filz, Gretchen, Catholic Company Magazine. "A Catholic's Guide to Halloween." The Catholic Company, 30 Oct. 2020, https://www.catholiccompany.com/magazine/a-catholics-guide-to-halloween/#. Accessed 29 March 2021.

History, The History.com-Editors. "Halloween." History, 30 October 2020, https://www.history.com/topics/halloween/history-of-halloween. Accessed 29 March 2021.

About the Author

Maria Felicia Kelley discovered her passion for writing as a girl growing up in the suburbs of Washington, DC. Earning a degree in broadcast journalism, from The Cronkite School at Arizona State University, María began her career in television as a writer and producer. She also has enjoyed time in front of the camera as a host and spokesperson. Today, she writes creatively with an eye toward children's stories and educational materials. The pandemic of 2020 moved María to focus her creative energy, bringing long-planned artistic works to life. Wife to a proud Greek American and mother to their three sons, María lives in a Southern California household with strong male energy and an assortment of ethnic identities. As a tri-racial mix, including African, European, and Native American bloods, María taps into the traditions of many cultures. Through much of her writing, she explores the intricacies of her family's racial heritage that is uniquely American.

About the Illustrator

Pratima Sarkar was born and raised in New Delhi, India. She started drawing freehand at a young age and later expanded her artistic skills while mastering the latest digital platforms. She earned her Bachelor of Arts degree from Delhi University. In 2006, she launched her career as a children's book illustrator. Pratima is a self-motivated artist who creates a range of multi-faceted art styles.

CPSIA information can be obtained
at www.ICGtesting.com
Printed in the USA
LVHW070002300921
699099LV00016B/838